RUBY BRIDGES
TAKES HER SEAT

COURAGEOUS KID OF THE CIVIL RIGHTS MOVEMENT

by Myra Faye Turner

illustrated by Dante Ginevra

CAPSTONE PRESS
a capstone imprint

Published by Capstone Press, an imprint of Capstone.
1710 Roe Crest Drive North Mankato, Minnesota 56003
capstonepub.com

Library of Congress Cataloging-in-Publication Data is available on the Library of Congress website.
ISBN: 9781666334340 (hardcover)
ISBN: 9781666334371 (paperback)
ISBN: 9781666334364 (ebook PDF)

Summary: When 6-year-old Ruby Bridges arrived at William Frantz Elementary School on November 14, 1960, she was met by an angry crowd of white people shouting racist insults. White parents pulled their children out of the school, and most of the white teachers refused to teach Ruby. But despite the hateful attitudes of others, Ruby didn't miss a single day of school that year. Discover Ruby's incredible bravery as she faced terrible persecution just to go to school with her fellow white students.

All internet sites appearing in back matter were available and accurate when this book was sent to press.

EDITOR
Aaron Sautter

DESIGNER
Brann Garvey

MEDIA RESEARCHER
Morgan Walters

PRODUCTION SPECIALIST
Polly Fisher

Direct quotations appear in **bold italicized text** on the following pages:

Page 10: from *Brown v. Board of Education of Topeka, 347 U.S. 483*, May 16, 1954. Justia U.S. Supreme Court, https://supreme.justia.com/cases/federal/us/347/483/.

Pages 13, 16, 19, 24, 25, 28, and 29: from *Through My Eyes*, by Ruby Bridges. New York: Scholastic, 1999.

TABLE OF CONTENTS

THE RACIAL DIVIDE

After the Civil War (1861–1865) ended, enslaved people were set free. But with this freedom came a new set of problems. How would they support themselves and their families?

The U.S. government helped. But it wasn't enough. Many families started sharecropping to survive. Under this agreement, families rented plots of land to farm. The farmers didn't pay money to rent the land. Instead, the landowners received a part of the farmer's harvest.

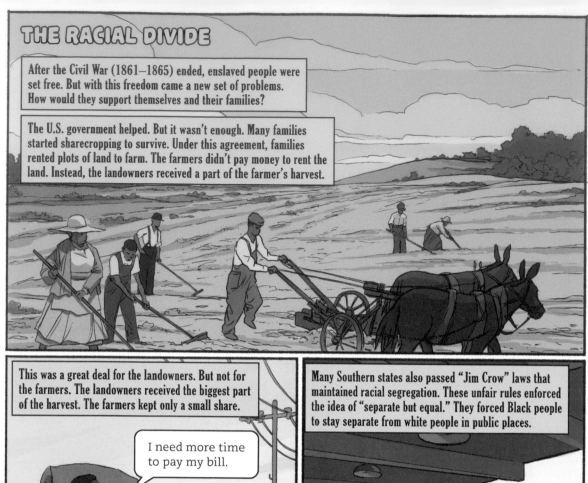

This was a great deal for the landowners. But not for the farmers. The landowners received the biggest part of the harvest. The farmers kept only a small share.

I need more time to pay my bill.

Okay, but I'll need a bigger share of your next harvest.

The farmers often got seeds and tools from the landowner with a promise to pay them back later. But after poor harvests, sharecroppers often couldn't pay their debts. They were stuck in a cycle of poverty.

Many Southern states also passed "Jim Crow" laws that maintained racial segregation. These unfair rules enforced the idea of "separate but equal." They forced Black people to stay separate from white people in public places.

Momma, I'm tired. Can we sit down?

This area is for white people only. You need to wait over there.

Under Jim Crow, businesses kept Black and white people apart. In movie theaters, Black people had to sit high in the balcony. White moviegoers had better seats on the main floor. Some businesses refused to serve Black customers at all.

Under Jim Crow, Black and white children couldn't even use the same water fountain.

I'm thirsty. Let's get a drink of water.

Not here. This is our fountain. You go drink from your own.

Black and white students also had to attend different schools.

In 1954, the U.S. Supreme Court ruled in the case *Brown v. Board of Education of Topeka Kansas* that Black and white students should go to school together.

But many schools in the South resisted, including schools in New Orleans, Louisiana.

Lawmakers there wrote new rules and went to court many times, but in the end they lost. White schools were forced to start admitting Black students in the fall of 1960.

END SCHOOL SEGREGATION!

INTEGRATION MEANS BETTER SCHOOLS

OUR KIDS DESERVE AN EDUCATION

END SCHOOL SEGREGATION!

OUR KIDS DESERVE EDUCATION

OUR KIDS DESERVE

At first, only a small group of Black first grade students were allowed to attend two all-white schools. One of those students was 6-year-old Ruby Bridges.

A BETTER LIFE

Ruby was born in Tylertown, Mississippi. She lived on a farm that her parents and paternal grandparents worked on as sharecroppers.

Ruby's maternal grandparents also lived in Mississippi. They were also sharecroppers who had a vegetable and dairy farm.

We need to finish planting this field by sundown.

This is going to be a long, hot day.

Sharecroppers worked long, hard days. They rarely took time off. On the day before Ruby was born, her mother carried 90 pounds of cotton on her back.

Ruby Nell Bridges was born September 8, 1954. She was the first of eight children born to Abon and Lucille Bridges.

In 1958, when Ruby was four years old, her family moved to New Orleans, Louisiana. Her parents wanted a better life for their growing family.

How much longer?

Not for a while yet, Ruby. We'll be there around lunchtime.

In New Orleans, an invisible line separated the neighborhood where Ruby and her family settled.

Black families lived on one side. White families lived on the other.

Ruby's parents soon found work in New Orleans. Her father worked at a gas station.

Her mother sometimes worked as a maid at a hotel and cleaned rooms at night.

During this time, the Civil Rights Movement was taking place. In 1960, almost 40 percent of the people in New Orleans were Black.

In spite of this, Black people faced discrimination daily. Activists often took to the streets to protest. Black customers could shop for clothes at department stores. However, they couldn't try them on. And the stores wouldn't give them jobs.

STOP SEGREGATION NOW!

WE SHALL OVERCOME

EQUAL

LET M GO T SCHO

Don't spend your money where you can't work!

Ruby didn't know about the protests. She was busy being a regular kid. But Ruby's carefree world would soon change.

9

SEPARATE, NOT EQUAL

When the U.S. Supreme Court ruled to end school segregation in the *Brown v. Board of Education* case, many whites in the South were angry.

TOM C. CLARK

FELIX FRANKFURTER

SHERMAN MINTON

HAROLD H. BURTON

ROBERT H. JACKSON

HUGO BLACK

STANLEY F. REED

WILLIAM O. DOUGLAS

The "separate but equal" doctrine . . . has no place in the field of public education."

CHIEF JUSTICE EARL WARREN

In New Orleans, segregationists wanted to keep the races separated. They filed lawsuits to prevent Black and white students from attending schools together. In the end, they lost the fight.

Please present your plan to desegregate the schools by May 1960.

JUDGE J. SKELLY WRIGHT

In 1956, a New Orleans judge ordered the school board to integrate the public schools. More lawsuits were filed with higher courts to stop his order. Finally in 1959, the original ruling was upheld.

However, the school board missed the deadline. So, in the fall of 1959, Ruby had to go to kindergarten at Johnson Lockett Elementary School.

All the students and teachers there were Black. The school was a long walk from her neighborhood.

Spring 1960

Integration in New Orleans would be gradual. For the first year, only two white schools would allow Black students, and those students could only be first graders. The schools were William Frantz Elementary School and McDonogh #19 Elementary School.

Where are we going mama?

Uptown.

Why?

You're going to take a test for school.

Before joining the schools, Black students had to first take a test. Their results would decide which students could attend the schools. But the test was unfairly designed so most Black students would fail.

About one hundred Black kindergartners took the test. Only a few passed it, including Ruby.

That summer, members of the National Association for the Advancement of Colored People (NAACP) came to the Bridges' home. The organization works to protect the civil rights of Black Americans.

The NAACP wanted Ruby's parents to send her to William Frantz Elementary.

It's a better school. Ruby will receive a better education there. And it's closer to your house.

It will help Ruby and your other kids. It will help all Black students.

I want Ruby to get a good education.

Yes, but I don't want Ruby to go anywhere she's not wanted. I don't think she'll be treated fairly.

And I don't want those white folks hurting my baby.

Ruby's parents decided to let her attend Frantz.

However, when school started that fall, she had to return to Johnson Lockett. Lawmakers in Baton Rouge, the state's capital, had blocked the court's ruling. Black students were once again not allowed to attend all-white schools.

JOHNSON LOCKETT PUBLIC SCHOOL

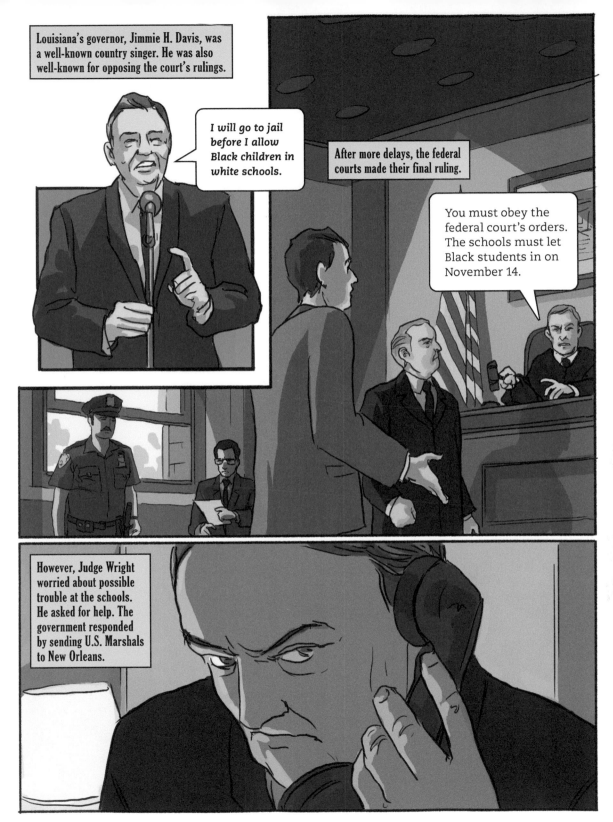

Louisiana's governor, Jimmie H. Davis, was a well-known country singer. He was also well-known for opposing the court's rulings.

I will go to jail before I allow Black children in white schools.

After more delays, the federal courts made their final ruling.

You must obey the federal court's orders. The schools must let Black students in on November 14.

However, Judge Wright worried about possible trouble at the schools. He asked for help. The government responded by sending U.S. Marshals to New Orleans.

13

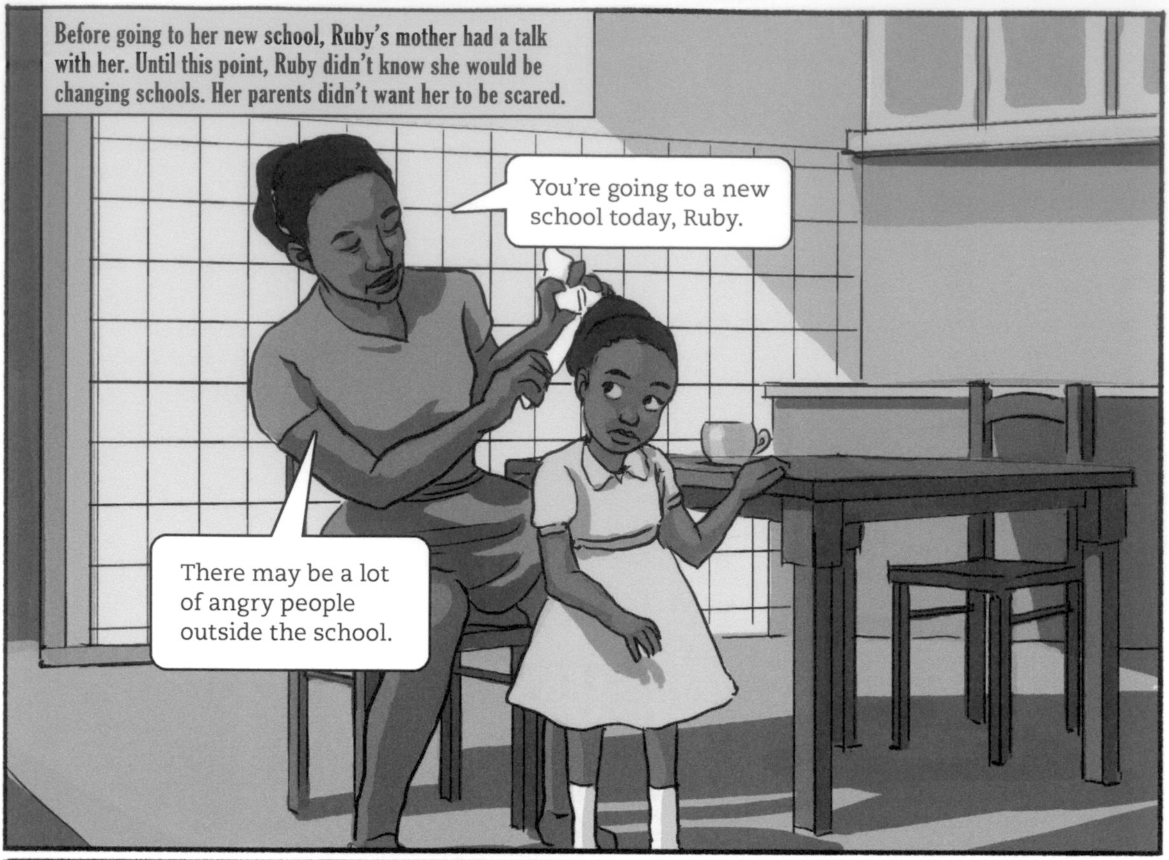
Before going to her new school, Ruby's mother had a talk with her. Until this point, Ruby didn't know she would be changing schools. Her parents didn't want her to be scared.
You're going to a new school today, Ruby.
There may be a lot of angry people outside the school.

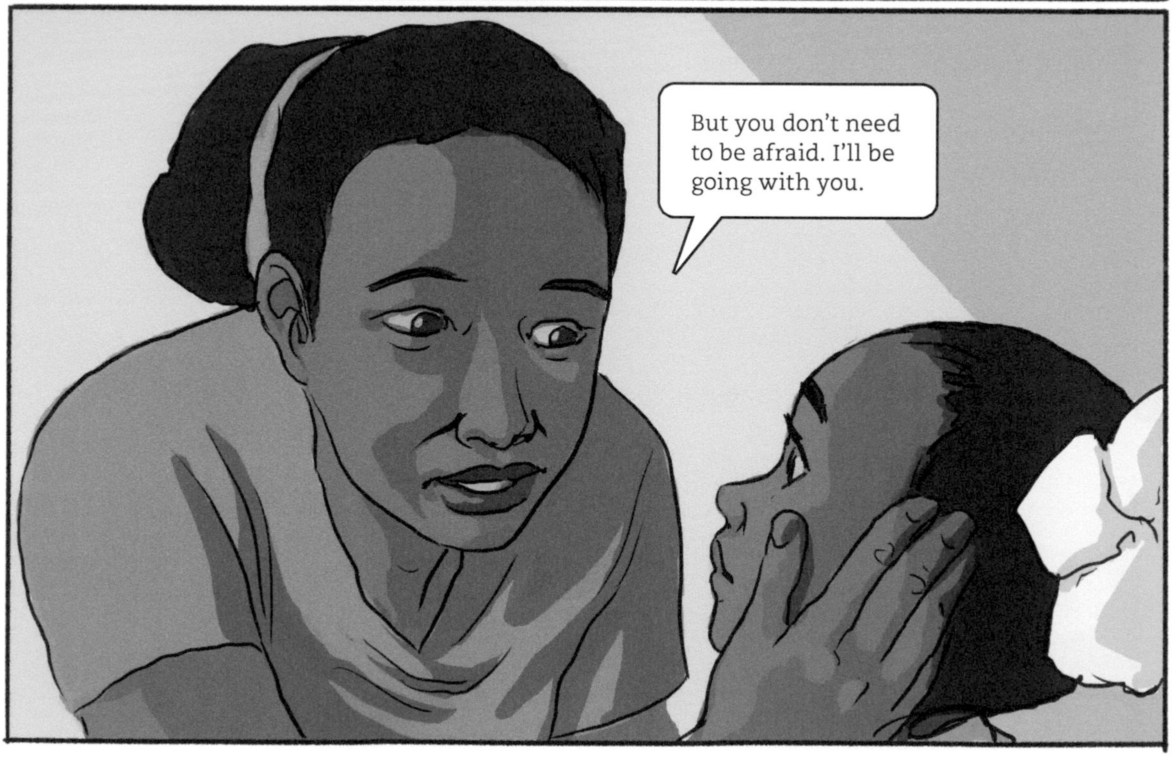
But you don't need to be afraid. I'll be going with you.

Six Black students were chosen to make history that day. But two of them decided to stay at their previous school. Three of the students would attend McDonogh #19 Elementary School.

RUBY BRIDGES

TESSIE PREVOST

LEONA TATE

GAIL ETIENNE

The students who dropped out would have gone to school with Ruby. But now, Ruby would be the only Black student at William Frantz Elementary School.

CIVIL UNREST

The morning of November 14, 1960

KNOCK! KNOCK!

William Frantz Elementary was only five blocks from the Bridges' home. Still, President Dwight D. Eisenhower sent men to protect Ruby.

Mrs. Bridges, I'm U.S. Marshal Charles Burks. We're here to escort you and Ruby to school.

The Marshals drove Ruby and her mother to school. Men from the neighborhood walked behind the car all the way there. The officers guarded Ruby inside.

Let us get out of the car first. Then you'll get out. The four of us will surround you and your daughter. We'll walk up to the door together. Just walk straight ahead, and don't look back.

A sea of angry white faces waited outside the school. When Ruby saw the crowd of protesters, she didn't know what to think.

Maybe it's Mardi Gras.

Two, four, six, eight—we don't want to integrate!

Just keep looking straight ahead Ruby.

RACE MIXING = COMMUNISM

BLACKS IN SCHOOLS!

Although she was allowed inside, the teachers at William Frantz refused to instruct Ruby. So she and her mother sat in the principal's office all day. The marshals sat in the hallway, just outside the principal's office.

By the end of the day, white parents had taken their kids out of school. At 3:00 p.m. Ruby was dismissed. The crowd outside had grown even larger.

We don't want your kind around here!

Go back to your own school!

On Ruby's second day of school, the angry crowd returned. One group of women were called "Cheerleaders." However, they didn't come to cheer for Ruby.

I'm going to poison you!

Once inside, the school's halls were very quiet. Ruby was the only student.

But there was some good news. She had a new teacher.

Hello Ruby. I'm your teacher, Mrs. Henry.

Hello.

Mrs. Barbara Henry and her husband had recently moved to New Orleans from Boston, Massachusetts. She had been a teacher and wanted to return to the classroom.

She soon applied for a teaching position. She then received a call from Dr. James Redmond, head of the New Orleans public school system.

Would you mind teaching an integrated class?

Of course not.

Mrs. Henry had already taught classes that included both Black and white students. She was willing to do so again.

Mrs. Henry led Ruby and her mother to an empty classroom on the second floor. The marshals sat outside the door. Ruby only left the classroom to use the restroom. When she did, an officer went with her.

AGAIN FIRST KIND
ALSO   FUNNY KNOW
CAKE   JUST

Let's go over some sight words. Do you know this word?

Cake.

Very good Ruby!

On Ruby's third day at Frantz, things would be different.

Ruby, I can't go to school with you today, but don't be afraid. The marshals will take care of you. Be good now, and don't cry.

SNIFFLE-SNIFFLE

Yes ma'am.

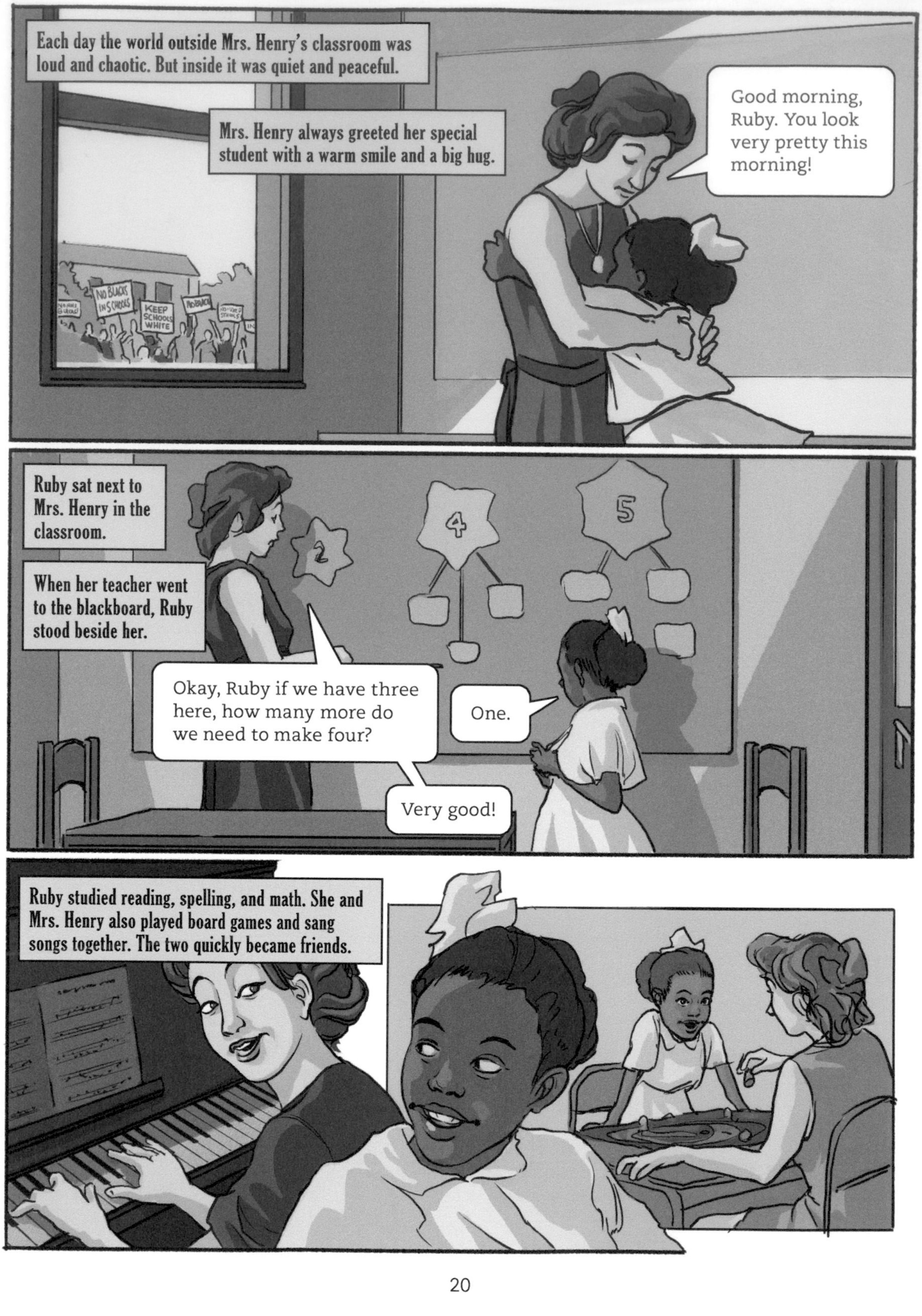
Each day the world outside Mrs. Henry's classroom was loud and chaotic. But inside it was quiet and peaceful.
Mrs. Henry always greeted her special student with a warm smile and a big hug.
NO BLACKS IN SCHOOLS
KEEP SCHOOLS WHITE
Good morning, Ruby. You look very pretty this morning!
Ruby sat next to Mrs. Henry in the classroom.
When her teacher went to the blackboard, Ruby stood beside her.
2
4
5
Okay, Ruby if we have three here, how many more do we need to make four?
One.
Very good!
Ruby studied reading, spelling, and math. She and Mrs. Henry also played board games and sang songs together. The two quickly became friends.

Ruby wasn't allowed to go outside. So, Mrs. Henry exercised with Ruby in the classroom.

One . . . two . . .

During the day, protests broke out across the city.

Keep our schools white!

We don't want Black kids in our schools!

At night, angry mobs burned crosses in Black neighborhoods.

How can I help?

Quick, grab a bucket. Run inside and get some water.

Meanwhile, the Bridges family experienced more discrimination. Mr. Bridges lost his job. And the local white grocery store owner refused to sell anything to the family.

We've been good customers. Where are we supposed to shop now?

I don't care. Y'all can't shop here. Not if you keep letting your daughter go to Frantz.

It wasn't all bad though. A neighbor offered Mr. Bridges a new job painting houses. The family received help from both neighbors and strangers. People from around the country sent money and gifts.

Ruby bravely went to school in spite of the angry crowds. But she was still only a little girl. She had bad dreams.

Mama, I had a bad dream.

Did you say your prayers?

No, ma'am.

Let's go say your prayers then. Everything will be okay.

22

Ruby started having eating problems too. At home, she only wanted to eat potato chips and drink soda. At school, Ruby hid her sandwich and milk.

One day child psychiatrist Dr. Robert Coles learned of Ruby's troubles. He later called the NAACP and offered to help Ruby.

Because of her age, it was hard for Ruby to voice her feelings using words. Dr. Coles told Ruby to draw pictures instead.

Ruby do you know why you've been having trouble eating?

No.

Is it because of the lady who said she would poison you? You don't have to be afraid. It's okay to eat your food.

STUDENT AND TEACHER

Despite the protests, a few white students soon returned to Frantz. However, the school secretly kept them away from Ruby and Mrs. Henry.

Rev. Lloyd Foreman brought his 5-year-old daughter Pam back.

I simply want the privilege of taking my child to school.

Yolanda Gabrielle also returned. Her family was harassed. Mr. Gabrielle lost his job. Three weeks later, the family left town.

Two, four, six, eight, we don't want to integrate.

What's going on in here?

Near the end of the school year, Mrs. Henry discovered the hidden, all-white first grade class.

I want Ruby and the other first graders to be together. By law, you have to integrate this school.

I won't force the other teacher to let that child into her class.

Mrs. Henry tried to explain integration to Ruby. She wasn't sure that Ruby understood. However, she wanted Ruby to know she wasn't to blame for what was happening. Ruby never complained. But Mrs. Henry knew she was lonely.

You are a wonderful and special person, Ruby. The other students will come back soon.

When?

I don't know.

At first, the principal refused to combine the classes. But Mrs. Henry threatened to tell the head of the school system about the principal's refusal. The principal agreed to allow the other students to come to Mrs. Henry's class for part of the day.

Finally, Ruby wasn't alone anymore.

The rest of the school year went by quickly. After the last day, Ruby and Mrs. Henry said their goodbyes.

It's been a joy to be your teacher, Ruby. Have a good summer.

Thank you Mrs. Henry. I'll miss you!

That summer zoomed by. Before long it was time for Ruby to start second grade. By then a few things had changed. The U.S. Marshals and the angry crowd were gone.

Sadly, Mrs. Henry was gone too. She was expecting a baby and had moved with her husband back to Boston. They decided they didn't want to raise their child in the South.

Ruby was sad. She thought Mrs. Henry was going to be her teacher again. Even worse, Ruby's new teacher wasn't very nice.

Both Black and white students were going to William Frantz Elementary. But not all the teachers were happy about it. Things had begun to change in the South. But it would take longer for some people to accept it.

Ruby Bridges was only six-years old when she made history. For months Ruby endured an angry mob as she made her way inside William Frantz Elementary. Inside, Ruby was her teacher's only student. But Mrs. Henry had made her feel special.

Ruby was scared at times. However, she remained brave despite the anger and hate. Ruby's courage was an inspiration to others. When she walked through the doors of Frantz, she made it possible for other Black students to soon follow. Ruby's brave deeds paved the way for future generations of Black students to have a better future.

FINDING HER VOICE

Ruby graduated from Francis T. Nicholls, an integrated high school. She later married and had four sons.

In 1964, artist Norman Rockwell made a famous painting of Ruby's historic first day at William Frantz Elementary.

Rockwell may have been inspired by a book about Ruby written by John Steinbeck. He wrote about Ruby walking through the angry crowd to the school. Rockwell's painting displays the courage Ruby showed that day.

THE PROBLEM WE ALL LIVE WITH

Today, Ruby is a Civil Rights icon. However, she didn't fully understand how important her role was to desegregation until she was an adult. When her younger brother was murdered in the early 1990s, Ruby took a long look at her own life.

Little by little, my life took on a new meaning.

Ruby's amazing courage as a child hasn't been forgotten. Dr. Robert Coles published a children's book about Ruby in 1995. In 1998 a feature film was made about the brave first grader.

In 1999, Ruby started the Ruby Bridges Foundation. It started as an after-school program at William Frantz Elementary.

Today Ruby travels around the country to speak about her experiences. She often talks to students about race problems in their own lives.

I soon realized that what I had done in 1960 was meaningful and important.

Ruby still lives in New Orleans.

Now that she's old enough, Ruby can share her story of overcoming her fears and helping Black students everywhere to be treated equally.

GLOSSARY

activist (AK-tih-vist)—someone who works for social or political change

chaotic (kay-AH-tik)—completely confused or disordered

civil rights (SI-vil RYTS)—the rights that all people have to freedom and equal treatment under the law

debt (DET)—money that is owed to someone

discrimination (dis-kri-muh-NAY-shuhn)—unfair treatment of a person or group, often because of race, country of birth, or gender

integrate (IN-tuh-grate)—to bring people of different races together in schools and other public places

maternal (muh-TUR-nuhl)—having to do with one's mother

paternal (puh-TUR-nuhl)—having to do with one's father

poverty (PAW-vuhr-tee)—the state of being poor or without money

psychiatrist (suh-KAHY-uh-trIst)—a doctor who treats patients with mental or emotional troubles

segregation (seg-ruh-GAY-shuhn)—the practice of keeping groups of people apart, especially based on their race

sharecropper (SHAIR-krop-ur)—a person who rents and farms a piece of land and pays the owner with money from the crops raised, or with part of the crops instead

READ MORE

Bridges, Ruby. *This is Your Time.* New York: Delacorte Press, 2020.

Clark-Robinson, Monica. *Let the Children March.* New York: Houghton Mifflin Harcourt, 2018.

Smith, Sherri. *What is the Civil Rights Movement?* New York: Penguin Workshop, 2020.

INTERNET SITES

Brown v. Board of Education of Topeka
kids.britannica.com/kids/article/Brown-v-Board-of-Education-of-Topeka/627788

Ruby Bridges
timeforkids.com/g56/ruby-bridges-2/

Ruby Bridges Facts for Kids
kids.kiddle.co/Ruby_Bridges

INDEX

ABOUT THE AUTHOR

Myra Faye Turner is a poet and author living in New Orleans, Louisiana. She has written for adults but prefers to write for young readers. She has written over two dozen nonfiction books for children and young adults. Topics covered include politics, the Apollo moon landing, edible insects, nature, STEM, firefighting robots, and U.S. and African-American history.